by Ellen Lawrence

Consultant:

Judy Wearing, PhD, BEd
Faculty of Education, Queen's University
Ontario, Canada

BEARPORT
PUBLISHING

New York, New York

Credits

Cover, © jakkapan/Shutterstock; 2–3, © CoraMax/Shutterstock, © Richard Petersen/Shutterstock, and © Valentina Razumova; 4–5, © Club4traveler/Shutterstock, © Be Good/Shutterstock, © Konstantin L/Shutterstock, © Rafal Olechowski/Shutterstock, © LeS/Shutterstock, © BlueOrange Studio/Shutterstock, and © Levranii/Shutterstock; 6–7, © CoraMax/Shutterstock, © Richard Petersen/Shutterstock, © Maxim Ibragimov/Shutterstock, and © Scisetti Alfio/Shutterstock; 8–9, © CoraMax/Shutterstock, © J. Palys/Shutterstock, © Richard Petersen/Shutterstock, © Sarah Marchant/Shutterstock, © warnsweet/Shutterstock, © vadimmmus/Shutterstock, © Imageman/Shutterstock, and © Ruby Tuesday Books; 10–11, © CoraMax/Shutterstock, © pixavril/Shutterstock, © Biehler Michael/Shutterstock, and © JGA/Shutterstock; 12–13, © CoraMax/Shutterstock, © endeavour/Shutterstock, © Joe Belanger/Shutterstock, and © JGA/Shutterstock; 14–15, © CoraMax/Shutterstock, © Ruby Tuesday Books, and © TigerForce/Shutterstock; 16–17, © CoraMax/Shutterstock, © Ruby Tuesday Books, © elenaburn/Shutterstock, © zhekoss/Shutterstock, © stocksolutions/Shutterstock, and © Artography/Shutterstock; 18–19, © CoraMax/Shutterstock and © Igor Karasi/Shutterstock; 20–21, © CoraMax/Shutterstock and © Ruby Tuesday Books; 22, © Tu Le/Shutterstock, © Siim Sepp/Shutterstock, © farbled/Shutterstock, and © isabela66/Shutterstock; 23, © kojihirano/Shutterstock, © Paul B. Moore/Shutterstock, © diplomedia/Shutterstock, © kamira/Shutterstock, © Richard Petersen/Shutterstock, © maxim ibragimov/Shutterstock, and © Marko Poplasen.

Publisher: Kenn Goin
Senior Editor: Joyce Tavolacci
Creative Director: Spencer Brinker
Design: Emma Randall
Photo Researcher: Ruby Tuesday Books Ltd.

Library of Congress Cataloging-in-Publication Data

Names: Lawrence, Ellen, 1967– author. | Lawrence, Ellen, 1967– FUNdamental experiments.
Title: Heat / by Ellen Lawrence.
Description: New York, New York : Bearport Publishing, [2016] | Series: FUN-damental experiments | Audience: Ages 7–12._ | Includes bibliographical references and index.
Identifiers: LCCN 2015037685 | ISBN 9781943553198 (library binding) | ISBN 194355319X (library binding)
Subjects: LCSH: Heat—Juvenile literature. | Thermodynamics—Juvenile literature.
Classification: LCC QC256 .L385 2016 | DDC 536.078—dc23
LC record available at http://lccn.loc.gov/2015037685

For more information, write to Bearport Publishing Company, Inc., 45 West 21st Street, Suite 3B, New York, NY 10010.
Printed in the United States of America.

10 9 8 7 6 5 4 3 2 1

Contents

Let's Investigate Heat

On a hot summer day, the sun's heat can warm your face and melt your ice cream. On a cold winter day, a mug of hot chocolate can heat up your icy-cold fingers. We feel and experience heat in different ways, but what exactly is heat? Inside this book are lots of fun experiments and facts about heat. So grab a notebook, and let's start investigating!

Check It Out!

Heat comes from many different **sources** including fire. People have used fire to keep warm for hundreds of thousands of years.

Think about other sources of heat.

▶ How many can you think of?

▶ How do people use heat in their daily lives?

Make a list in a notebook.

What happens when hot meets cold?

Heat is a form of **energy**. When something is hot, it has lots of heat energy. When something is cold, it has less heat energy. Heat energy can **transfer** from one object to another. When this happens, hot things usually cool down and cold things warm up. Let's find out more about heat transfer in this investigation.

You will need:

- An ice cube
- A small bowl
- A notebook and a pencil

 Place an ice cube in a small bowl. Touch the ice cube with your finger for a few seconds.

▸ How does your finger feel?

▸ What do you think is happening?

Write down your ideas in your notebook.

2 Now pick up the ice cube and hold it in your hand for a few seconds.

▶ How does your hand feel?

▶ What do you observe happening to the ice?

There were two objects in your experiment—an ice cube and your hand.

▶ Which object lost heat, and which object gained heat?

▶ What evidence do you have to support your answer?

(To learn more about this investigation and find the answers to the questions, see pages 20–21.)

How does heat energy affect tiny units called molecules?

Almost everything is made up of tiny units called **molecules**—including water, this book, and even you! Molecules are much too tiny to see. In fact, there are billions of molecules in just one drop of water. In addition to being small, molecules are always on the move. They jostle around and bump into each other. In this experiment, you will investigate how heat energy affects molecules!

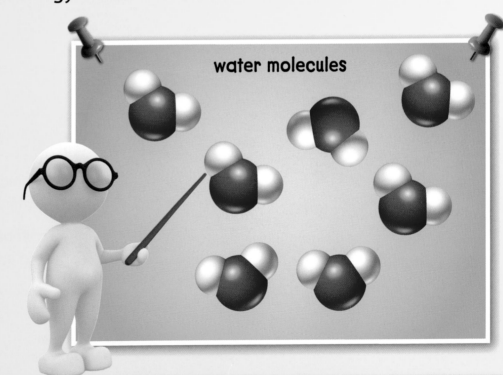

water molecules

You will need:

- Three clear glass jars
- A marker
- Labels
- Ice water (with the ice cubes removed)
- Cool tap water
- An adult helper
- Very hot tap water
- Food coloring
- A notebook and a pencil

Take the three jars and label them A, B, and C.

Fill jar A with ice water. Fill jar B with cool tap water. Ask an adult to fill jar C with very hot tap water. The water molecules in each jar are moving—even if you cannot see them.

 Add five drops of food coloring to each jar.

▶ What do you think will happen to the food coloring in each jar?

Write your **predictions** in your notebook, and then observe what happens.

In your notebook, write down everything you observed.

▶ What happened to the food coloring in each jar?

▶ How do you think heat energy affects molecules?

(To learn more about this investigation and find the answers to the questions, see pages 20–21.)

9

Can heat change solids to liquids?

You've discovered that heat can melt ice, but can it change other solid materials from one state to another? Let's investigate!

You will need:

- A square of chocolate
- A cold cube of butter
- A cube of hard cheese
- A piece of wax crayon
- A notebook and a pencil
- Four small foil dishes
- An adult helper
- A baking tray
- Hot tap water

1 Begin by examining the chocolate, butter, cheese, and crayon.

▶ How do the solids feel when you touch them?

▶ How do you think heat will change these materials?

Write your predictions in your notebook.

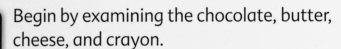

2 Place each of the materials into a separate foil dish.

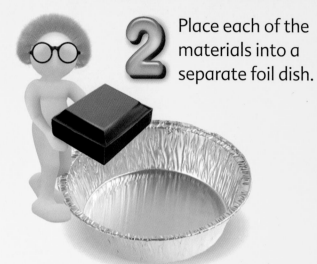

4 Carefully place the four foil dishes in the baking tray. Then observe what happens.

> ▶ What did you observe happening to each of the materials?
>
> ▶ Which solids changed?
>
> ▶ How did they change?

(To learn more about this investigation and find the answers to the questions, see pages 20–21.)

3 Ask an adult to help you fill a baking tray with hot tap water.

Which material spreads heat the best?

The movement of heat is called **conduction**. Conduction doesn't only happen between objects. Heat energy is also transferred from molecule to molecule inside objects. Some materials are good conductors, while others are poor conductors. In this next investigation, we'll explore how well different materials conduct heat.

You will need:

- A metal spoon, a wooden spoon, and a plastic spoon that are all about the same length
- A notebook and a pencil
- A butter knife
- Very cold butter
- An adult helper
- A bowl
- Very hot tap water

 Examine each of the three spoons.

▶ Which spoon do you think will conduct heat the best? Why?

Write your predictions in your notebook.

 Ask an adult to cut three small, grape-sized pieces of butter. Then press a piece of butter into each of the three spoons. The butter should stick to the spoons.

Stand the handles of the three spoons in the bowl. Ask an adult to carefully pour very hot tap water into the bowl. The water should come about halfway up the handles of the spoons.

Then observe what happens.

In your notebook, write down everything you observed.

▸ What happened to the butter on each of the spoons?

▸ What do you think was happening to the spoons?

▸ Which spoon conducted heat the best? Which spoon was the worst conductor?

(To learn more about this investigation and find the answers to the questions, see pages 20–21.)

Which materials stop heat from spreading?

Not all materials are good at conducting heat. Materials that are very poor conductors can be used to stop the transfer of heat from one object to another. These materials are called **insulators**. Let's investigate which materials are good insulators.

You will need:

- An adult helper
- Scissors
- A ruler
- A plastic bag or plastic wrap
- Wax paper
- Wool or felt
- Aluminum foil
- Four ice cubes
- A dinner plate
- A notebook and a pencil

1 Ask an adult to help you cut 4-inch by 4-inch (10 cm x 10 cm) squares from the following materials. Examine each square of material.

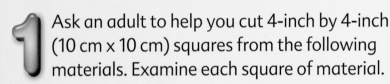

plastic bag

wax paper

wool

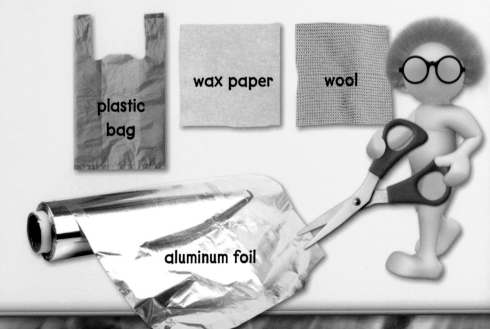

aluminum foil

2 Wrap each ice cube with one of the four materials. Then place the wrapped ice cubes on a plate in a sunny or warm place.

▶ Which ice cube do you think will melt first? Why?

▶ Which material or materials do you think will insulate the ice cubes the best?

 3 After 15 minutes, unwrap the ice cubes and compare their sizes.

In your notebook, write down everything you observed.

▶ Which ice cube has melted the most? How about the least?

▶ Make a list that shows how good the materials you used were at insulating. Label the best material *number 1* and the worst *number 4*.

▶ Which material was the worst insulator? Why do you think this is?

(To learn more about this investigation and find the answers to the questions, see pages 20–21.)

How much does the sun heat up Earth's land and water?

The main source of heat on Earth is the sun. Without the sun's heat and light, people, animals, plants, and other living things could not survive. On a sunny day, you can feel the sun's heat on your skin, but how much does the sun heat up Earth's land and water? Let's investigate by using a **thermometer**!

You will need:

- Four small white bowls
- Potting soil
- Water
- Two thermometers
- A notebook and a pencil

1 Fill two bowls with potting soil. Fill the other two bowls with water.

2 Put one thermometer into a bowl of potting soil, and put the other thermometer into a bowl of water. After a few minutes, check the thermometers and record in your notebook the starting temperature of the soil and the water.

Remove the thermometers, and then put one bowl of soil and one bowl of water in a shady spot outside.

 Place the other bowls of soil and water in a sunny spot outside.

▶ How do you think the temperature of each bowl will change?

Write your predictions in your notebook.

 After 30 minutes, measure and record the temperature of all four bowls.

▶ How did the temperature of the bowls of soil and water change after they were placed in the sun and in the shade?

(To learn more about this investigation and find the answers to the questions, see pages 20–21.)

Can rubbing objects together produce heat?

We've discovered that heat is produced by the sun. We also get heat from fire and from radiators and stoves. Our bodies also **generate** heat, but is it possible to make heat in another way? For example, can we generate heat by rubbing two objects together? Let's investigate!

You will need:

- A notebook and a pencil
- Hand lotion

 Put your hands on your cheeks.

▶ How do your hands feel? Are they cold or warm?

Record how your hands feel in your notebook.

2 Rub your hands together hard as you count to 20. Then place your hands on your cheeks.

▶ How do your hands feel now?

▶ What do you think caused this change?

4 Rub your hands together hard while counting to 20. Place your hands on your cheeks.

▶ How warm do your hands feel compared to the last time you rubbed them and placed them on your cheeks?

3 Place a small amount of hand lotion on one palm.

▶ Do you think the lotion will make it easier or harder to rub your hands together?

▶ How do you think the lotion will affect how warm your hands get?

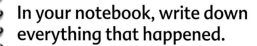

In your notebook, write down everything that happened.

▶ Did rubbing your hands together generate heat?

▶ What do you think happened to the molecules in your hands when you rubbed your hands together?

▶ What changed when you put lotion on your hands? Why do you think this is?

(To learn more about this investigation and find the answers to the questions, see pages 20–21.)

Discovery Time

Using science to investigate heat is fun!
Now, let's check out all the things we've discovered.

What happens when hot meets cold?

Pages 6-7

The heat was transferred from your hand to the ice cube. Your hand lost heat and the ice cube gained heat. Your hand felt cold because heat from your hand was transferring to the ice cube. The ice cube started to melt because it was gaining heat. It might feel as if cold from the ice cube was transferring to your hand, but that's not what happens. Heat always transfers from a warmer object to a colder one.

How does heat energy affect tiny units called molecules?

Pages 8-9

The food coloring quickly spread throughout the hot water in jar C. That's because molecules move faster when they're heated. As the molecules of hot water zipped around, they quickly spread the food coloring through the water. The food coloring in jar A did not spread as much. That's because the molecules of ice water were moving slowly. The water in jar B was neither very cold nor very hot. The food coloring in jar B spread faster than in jar A, but slower than in jar C.

Can heat change solids to liquids?

Pages 10-11

The heat from the hot water transferred to the foil dishes and then to the materials inside the dishes. All solids have a melting point. This is the temperature at which things change from a solid to a liquid. The heat from the water caused the chocolate and butter to reach their melting points. However, there was not enough heat to change the cheese and wax crayon. That's because these materials have higher melting points. So heat can turn a solid to a liquid, but different solids melt at different temperatures.

Which material spreads heat the best?

The butter on the metal spoon melted quickly. This is because heat from the water conducted through the metal spoon. Water and metal are both good conductors of heat. Then the heat transferred to the cold butter, which grew warm and melted. The pieces of butter on the wooden spoon and plastic spoon probably didn't melt. This is because wood and plastic are poor conductors of heat.

Pages 12-13

Which materials stop heat from spreading?

The ice cube wrapped in aluminum foil melted the most. This is because the foil is made of metal, which is a good conductor of heat. However, that also means it's a bad insulator. The ice cubes wrapped in felt or wool melted the least. These materials were the best at insulating the ice cubes.

Pages 14-15

Insulators tested:
1. Felt or wool
2. Wax paper
3. Plastic wrap or plastic bag
4. Aluminum foil

How much does the sun heat up Earth's land and water?

The temperature of the soil and water in the bowls that were placed in the sun will be higher. This is because heat from the sun has transferred to the soil and water. Just as the sun warms the land and water on Earth, it also warms the soil and water in the bowls. The soil and water in the shade may have stayed the same temperature or even gotten cooler. This is because little of the sun's light and heat reached the shaded bowls.

Pages 16-17

sun   shade

Can rubbing objects together produce heat?

By rubbing your hands together hard, you generated **friction**. This is a force that's produced when two surfaces try to move against each other. The friction made the molecules in your hands move faster and faster, generating heat. When you put lotion on your hands, it made them slippery and reduced the amount of friction. Less friction meant less heat was generated, so your hands did not feel as warm.

Pages 18-19

Heat in Your World

You've discovered a lot about heat in the science experiments in this book. Now, check out the ways you can see heat energy in action every day!

1. When you go outside on a cold winter day, your face feels cold.

▶ **Why do you think this is?**

2. When you put ice cubes in a drink, they start to melt because heat is transferring to the ice cubes.

▶ **Where does the heat come from?**

3. Before a pizza is baked, the cheese on top is solid.

▶ **What makes the cheese on the pizza become soft and stringy after it's baked?**

4. Many saucepans and frying pans are made of metal. Their handles, however, are made of wood or plastic.

▶ **Why do you think the handles are not made from metal?**

Answers: **1.** Heat from your body is transferring to the cold air around you. Your face feels cold because it's losing heat. **2.** The heat is transferring from the drink. The drink may not feel as if it has heat, but it has more heat than the ice cubes. So heat transfers from the warmer object, to the colder one, the ice cubes. **3.** When a pizza is put into a hot oven, the solid cheese reaches its melting point. It stops being solid and becomes soft and runny. **4.** The part of a pan where the food is cooked is made of metal so that heat conducts to the food. A pan's handle is made of wood or plastic because these materials are poor conductors of heat. This stops heat from conducting to the handle and burning a person's hand.

Science Words

conduction (kuhn-DUHK-shuhn) the process by which heat spreads or is transferred through an object or between objects

energy (EN-ur-jee) power that can come from different sources, for example, heat from the sun

friction (FRIK-shuhn) the force that is created when two surfaces move against each other

generate (JEN-ur-ayt) to make

insulators (IN-suh-layt-urz) materials that are good at blocking heat transfer

molecules (MOL-uh-kyoolz) tiny parts that make up everything

predictions (pri-DIK-shuhnz) guesses that something will happen in a certain way; they are often based on facts a person knows or something a person has observed

sources (SORSS-iz) the places from which something comes; for example, fire is a source of heat

thermometer (thur-MOM-uh-tur) an instrument that measures the temperature of something

transfer (TRANS-fur) to move from one place to another

Index

Read More

Stille, Darlene R. *Temperature: Heating Up and Cooling Down.* Minneapolis, MN: Picture Window Books (2004).

Thomas, Isabel. *Experiments with Heating and Cooling (Read and Experiment).* Mankato, MN: Heinemann Raintree (2015).

Walker, Sally M. *Heat (Early Bird Energy).* Minneapolis, MN: Lerner (2006).

Learn More Online

To learn more about heat, visit
www.bearportpublishing.com/FundamentalExperiments

About the Author

Ellen Lawrence lives in the United Kingdom. Her favorite books to write are those about nature and animals. In fact, the first book Ellen bought for herself, when she was six years old, was the story of a gorilla named Patty Cake that was born in New York's Central Park Zoo.